JAPANESE MYTHOLOGY

JUDITH LEVIN

rosen publishing's
rosen central®

New York

For Laura, of course

Published in 2008 by The Rosen Publishing Group, Inc.
29 East 21st Street, New York, NY 10010

Copyright © 2008 by The Rosen Publishing Group, Inc.

First Edition

Library of Congress Cataloging-in-Publication Data

Levin, Judith.
Japanese mythology / Judith Levin.—1st ed.
    p. cm.—(Mythology around the world)
Includes bibliographical references and index.
ISBN-13: 978-1-4042-0736-3
ISBN-10: 1-4042-0736-8
1. Mythology, Japanese.
I. Title. II. Series.
BL2203.L48 2007
299.5'6—dc22

2005035279

Manufactured in the United States of America

On the cover: In Shinto, Amaterasu, the sun goddess, is believed to be the ancestor of the rulers of Japan.

CONTENTS

INTRODUCTION

In Japanese mythology, gods are born from the eyes or noses of other gods. They marry their brothers or sisters. They produce food out their rectums. They get mad and chop one another up into pieces. One god yanks down her clothing and performs a dance in front of the other gods and they all crack up laughing.

None of this is precisely the behavior the Japanese people expect from themselves, however. In fact, Japanese people often behave quite conservatively and are famous for valuing courtesy, restraint, and cleanliness. Yet outrageous behavior is pretty normal in Japanese mythology. The behavior of the gods is strange at best, and sometimes disgusting. It usually does not set a direct example for human beings of how to behave. Sometimes the message seems to be that the gods do not have traits that are human. While they may be described as though they are human, they are not. In many creation myths, for example, gods exist in a realm quite different from the one in which humans inhabit. In these myths, gods live in a world that existed before creation, before the sun and the moon, and before the land and the sea. It represents a time before the laws of nature existed and before human laws and customs existed either.

Japan's name in Japanese, Nihon or Nippon, comes from the Chinese characters that mean "origin of the sun." Japan is to the east of China—the direction from which the sun rises. According to Japanese myth, the Japanese people are the children of the

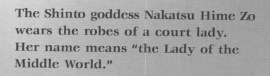

The Shinto goddess Nakatsu Hime Zo wears the robes of a court lady. Her name means "the Lady of the Middle World."

sun goddess Amaterasu. The flag of Japan is white with a solid red circle on it. That red circle represents the sun.

Japan's native religion, Shinto, is based upon the worshipping of many gods and spirits; the word *Shinto* means "the way of the kami." In Japanese, gods are known as *kami*, and they are believed to inhabit every living thing, including humans, as well as nonliving things like rocks, trees, waterfalls, or buildings. Many of the stories that make up Japan's mythology revolve around the sun goddess Amaterasu.

1 JAPAN

Perhaps the most important thing to remember about Japan is that it is an island nation: an archipelago of small, mountainous islands possessing few natural resources. Unlike many modern countries, Japan is largely homogeneous ethnically: almost all the people there share the same heritage and customs.

Throughout their history, the Japanese have learned things from other cultures and then made these things their own. They learned writing and centralized government and

This clay statue of a warrior was buried in an ancient tomb around 500 CE when Japan was first unified as a country. Its job was to guard the tomb and the person buried in it.

Buddhism from the Chinese in the 500s. They learned technology from the United States and Europe in the nineteenth century and again in the twentieth. Anything they learn—how to manufacture automobiles or cellular phones, for example, or how to figure skate or play baseball—they rapidly do as well as, or better than, whomever they learned it from. The Japanese are famous for this trait.

Historically, periods of intense learning in Japan have alternated with periods of withdrawal from the rest of the world. During these times, Japan takes advantage of being an island nation. It shuts itself from other countries and rediscovers its own identity, as it did between the beginning of the 1600s and the middle of the 1800s. For 250 years, the Tokugawa shogunate banned travel to foreign countries and all trade with Europe and the United States.

Having adopted Buddhism as a religion and added it to Shinto, the native Japanese religion, Japan attempted in the nineteenth century to reject Buddhism and reestablish Shinto. This was in part a response to Japan's having had its national doors pried open by the West: In 1853, Commodore Matthew Perry arrived with a fleet of ships and forced Japan to open trade relations with the United States, and then with Europe. Emperor Meiji, who was then restored to power after years of military dictatorships, decided it was time to modernize. He wanted Japan to compete economically in the industrializing world, but he still did not want the Japanese to lose their identity. What resulted was a period of strong nationalism and the use by the government of certain elements of traditional Japanese mythology. One of these myths said that the emperor was

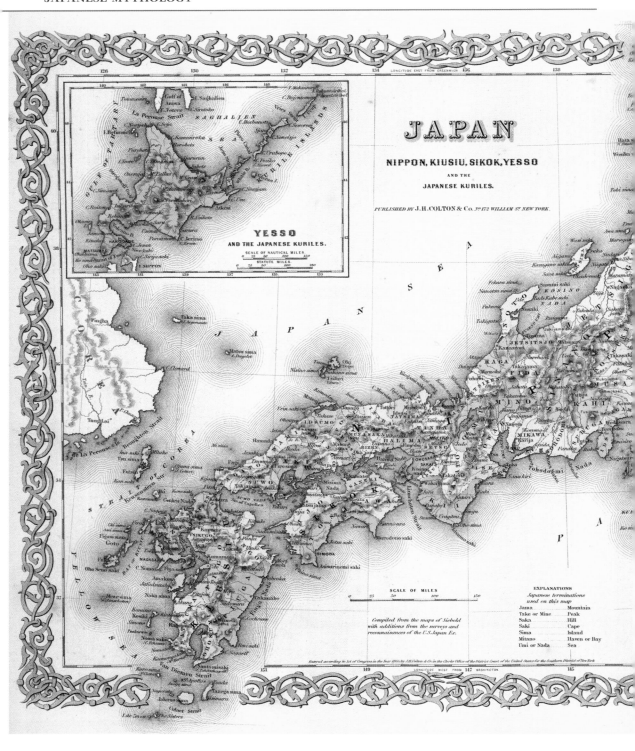

JAPAN

NIPPON, KIUSIU, SIKOK, YESSO

AND THE

JAPANESE KURILES.

PUBLISHED BY J.H.COLTON & Co. N° 172 WILLIAM S? NEW YORK.

YESSO
AND THE JAPANESE KURILES.

SCALE OF NAUTICAL MILES.

STATUTE MILES.

EXPLANATIONS
Japanese terminations
used on this map

Jama	Mountain
Take or Mine	Peak
Saka	Hill
Saki	Cape
Sima	Island
Mitano	Haven or Bay
Uni or Nada	Sea

SCALE OF MILES

Compiled from the maps of Siebold
with additions from the surveys and
reconnaisances of the U.S.Japan Ex.

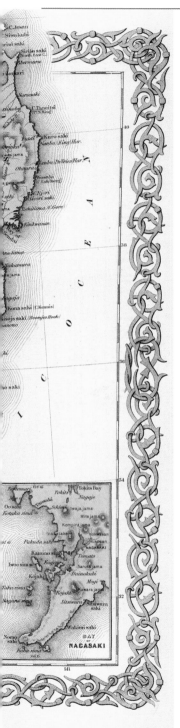

the direct descendant of the goddess of the sun and was himself a god. This myth reiterated that Japan was a superior nation because of its lineage. For a time, this myth was also understood to mean that the emperor had a right to rule the world.

Industrialized Japan

Japanese businesses flourished, and so did its economy. Japan industrialized rapidly. In just a few years, it successfully went from being an agricultural nation to one with the highest gross national product (GNP) in the world. Then, during World War II, Japan fought on the side of the Axis powers, with Germany and against the United States and Russia. Japan entered the war in a dramatic way on December 7, 1941, by bombing the United States naval base at Pearl Harbor. The bombing killed more than 2,000 American sailors and brought America into the war. Japan surrendered only after the

Published in an atlas in 1856, soon after Commodore Matthew Perry opened Japan to the West, this would have been the first map of Japan most Westerners would have seen.

9

This Buddhist temple, built between 1397 and 1398, is covered with real gold. The Kinkaku-ji, which means "Golden Pavilion," is in Kyoto.

United States returned the aggression and dropped atomic bombs on the Japanese cities of Hiroshima and Nagasaki. Emperor Hirohito renounced his claim to being a god and Shinto was ended as the official national religion. The Japanese again industrialized with such speed and efficiency that many people are still writing books trying to figure out how they did it. Yet, throughout all the periods when the state decreed a religion, the Japanese have continued to tell their myths to each generation and continued to visit Shinto shrines and Buddhist temples.

2 THE MAGIC OF MYTHOLOGY

Much of what makes a culture unique is its traditions. A culture's ways of eating, speaking, dressing, and celebrating holidays are passed down from one generation to another, by word of mouth, in writing, or by example. These traditions may change through time, as technology advances or as cultures are influenced by one another, but it is still possible to see distinct patterns in the traditional behavior of a people.

Hotei is one of the seven Buddhist gods of fortune. In this ink painting, a Buddhist would recognize Hotei, even though he is not in the picture. His bag, stick, and fan (which *are* in the picture) would be enough to identify him.

Storytelling is one important part of traditional culture. These stories can be about heroes or villains, creation or destruction, great battles won or lost, epic journeys, or the adventures of children or animals. A myth is a special kind of story.

Myths, Legends, Folktales, and Fairy Tales

Often, though not always, people recognize a difference between true stories and stories that the teller and the audience know are told for entertainment. Yet even stories that aren't true communicate values. We don't think stories like that of Cinderella are true; still, we know that the story tells us that Cinderella's behavior is preferable to her sisters' behavior—especially in the German version in which little birds peck out the eyes of Cinderella's sisters. Fairy tales, like legends and myths, offer an insight into the ways in which we feel about ourselves and the people and the world around us.

Myths are another kind of story, originally passed down orally, by word of mouth. People who study traditional stories sometimes say that the difference between a myth and a folktale is that a myth is told as true. Myths are stories that people believe or at least that the people of their culture tell them to believe. As opposed to a legend, like those about Paul Bunyan or Johnny Appleseed, a myth may be set in the distant past, in a time before the world existed as it does now. Myths may contain information about gods or supernatural beings, or interactions between gods and humans. Myths often explain how things came to be the way they are now and answer

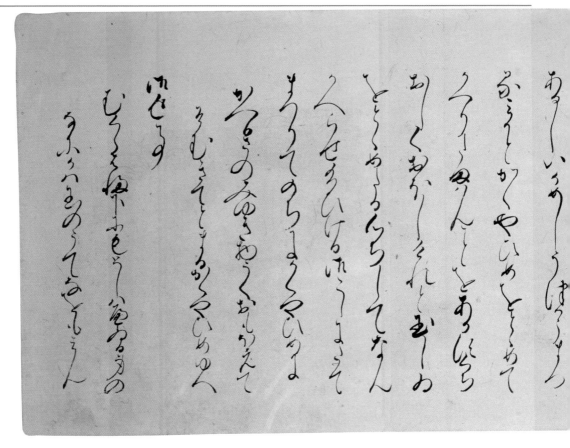

In the Japanese folktale "The Tale of the Bamboo Cutter," many suitors approach a beautiful girl with shining hair, but she must return to her own people, on the moon. The story is still popular in Japan and has been made into movies.

questions about the origin of Earth and of life: Where did the world come from? How did the sun and the moon come to inhabit the sky? Why do people have to die? What happens to us after death? Why are there men and women?

Myths that account for how the world is ordered, how it began, and, often, the place of human beings in the grand scheme of things are cosmologies, or cosmogonies, from the Greek word *kosmos*

meaning "order." Myths tell people how to behave toward a god or gods and toward one another. They explain why people celebrate certain holidays or conduct certain rites (traditional activities or ceremonies like those associated with birth, becoming an adult, marriage, and death). Myths are often about matters that are mysterious and unknowable. Often, though not always, they are sacred and are related to a culture's religion.

Around the end of the 1700s, the artist Torii Kiyonaga created this image of a Japanese ritual: the marriage ceremony.

Myths also deal with heroes who may be part human and part divine. Some Japanese myths after the introduction of Buddhism tell of great Zen masters, warriors, or monks. They, like the Buddha himself, are historical figures who become supernatural, which poses no problem for a culture in which people became gods after death anyway.

Interpreting Mythology Through the Ages

If your first thought when you hear the word "myth" is "falsehood," you might be interested in knowing that the Greek philosopher Plato said it before you did. In the early fourth century BCE, Plato contrasted rational argument with mythic thought. Plato believed that mythology was the opposite of reason. Today's understanding that a myth is an incorrect explanation for a scientific or historical event comes from Plato and the ancient Greeks. The thinking of the Greek philosophers paved the way for the modern scientific method and for a way of looking at and examining evidence. It did not bring myth or religion to an end, however, or even stop myths from developing since Christianity and Islam became world religions after Plato, but it suggested a different way of asking and answering questions about the creation of the world.

The tension between these ways of examining the world has remained important throughout the ages. During the seventeenth and eighteenth centuries, a time known as the Age of Enlightenment, scientific thinkers again rejected myths. Thinkers of the Enlightenment believed mythology got in the way of genuine inquiry. Why did people believe such stories? they wondered. After considering the newly "discovered" (and conquered) peoples of the New World, scholars suggested that mythology represented a kind of universal "childhood of man," when cultures created myths to explain things they otherwise could not understand.

It is not only the Japanese people who have stories to explain
their origins. A 1534 Bible included this picture of God creating
Adam and Eve, the Garden of Eden, and the sun, moon, stars,
and sky around them.

Why Are Myths from Distant Cultures Similar?

In the eighteenth and nineteenth centuries, scholars studying the myths of various cultures began to wonder why myths showed so many similarities even though the cultures themselves were so different. Did all the myths begin in one part of the world and then travel with various cultures as they migrated and merged? India was suggested as one possible geographical point for the source of world mythology. At that time, scholars interested in learning the origin of language were trying to explain the similarities among many European and Near Eastern languages. The scholars traced the languages back to an earlier Indian language and then documented how it had changed as it developed. Some scholars believed that the spread of cultures accounts for the similarities among mythologies. In some instances, this is correct. Some Asian myths resemble one another because the cultures were exchanging those stories.

Another way of explaining the similarities in myths was suggested in the twentieth century by psychoanalyst Sigmund Freud. He suggested that myths (and dreams) represent in symbols the basic aspects of human experience. Freud believed that the most basic forces in human nature are aggression and love. To Freud and to his student, Carl Jung, myths were not leftovers from the "childhood of man" and the similarities in myths were not due to their having spread from one original source. Freud believed that myths were vital and necessary expressions of essential parts of the human mind and the human experience.

A Shared Human Experience

Anthropologists and folklorists—social scientists who study cultures and their traditions—look at myths as a reflection of the basic values of the culture in which they are told. If, as it seems, most cultures have needed to account for the origins of the world and of the place of human beings in that creation, what do the specific stories of these events tell us about the culture? What do the myths tell the people about themselves? In what way do the myths tell people what to value and how to live? This approach asks about differences among mythologies as well as their similarities. Human beings are born, grow up, grow old, and die; we love and hate our families; we see the sun come up in the morning and we wonder at the vastness of the stars. And yet cultures celebrate and mourn in different ways. They disagree about whether evil is basic to human nature or whether people are basically good. They emphasize the individual more than the group or vice versa. They understand gods, humans, and animals to be quite different with a clear hierarchy among them, or they understand a world in which gods dwell in every rock and rodent. The study of a culture's myths is one way to look at these differences. In doing so, we can try to understand how other peoples see their world.

3 JAPANESE MYTHOLOGY

Before they had writing, perhaps beginning around 300 BCE, the Japanese told stories of the kami. The kami are not gods in the way that Zeus is a god. Kami are not necessarily separate from the world or from people. They are, wrote scholar Motoori Norinaga (1730–1801), "deities of heaven and earth" but also spirits honored at shrines, "as well as the humans, birds and beasts, plants and trees, oceans and mountains that have exceptional

This fierce-looking man with a bow and arrow is a Buddhist or Shinto "guardian figure," who would have been stationed outside a temple door to protect the people within.

power and ought to be revered. Kami include not only mysterious beings that are noble and good but also malignant spirits that are extraordinary and deserve veneration." Anything that inspires feelings of awe, anything unusual in nature—a waterfall, an ocean, an unusually shaped rock—houses a kami. Thunder is the kami that rumbles. The emperor is a kami and so are one's ancestors. Even an object made by human beings, like a boat, may contain a kami. In fact, everything is potentially a kami. "I do not yet understand the meaning of the term kami," Norinaga admitted, having studied the matter at length.

During ancient times, honoring the kami was not part of an organized religion. Japan was a series of islands and it had no central government. Social organization was based on clans, tribes, and extended families. People tilled the land, planted rice, and honored the kami at shrines and in their homes. Probably many of the kami were known only to the family that honored them or to the people of one town. One of the ancient Japanese chronicles says, "In their world myriad spirits shone like fireflies and every tree and bush could speak."

We know that around the third or fourth century CE, the Japanese people told stories and built shrines to some important kami. One is the shrine of Amaterasu, the kami of the sun. She, like the kami of the moon and storm and others—the "kamis of the heavenly plain"—more closely resemble the ancient gods of the Romans or Aztecs. They are very powerful, not of the earth, and immortal. A shrine in Ise contains the Sacred Mirror, which has an important role in a myth about Amaterasu.

Shinto

Honoring the kami became known as Shinto—which simply means "the way of the kami"—only after it needed to be distinguished from Buddhism, which was brought to Japan from Korea in 522 CE. By this time, writing had been introduced from China, and the stories of the kami were written down as well as passed along by word of mouth. However, the earliest text we have of Shinto stories is from 712 CE. Written at the emperor's request, it is called *Kojiki*, or "Record of Ancient Matters." It includes myths about the creation of the world and of the islands of Japan, the origins of the sun and moon, and how death came into the world. The *Kojiki* also explains the necessity of washing and ritual purification, both essential to Shinto and to Japanese culture.

Shinto is a religion that concentrates on our life in this world. Although its myths speak of the heavens (the High Plain of Heaven, from where the original gods came) and of an underworld (the Dark Land, an unclean place), they did not resemble a Christian heaven or hell. Neither is a place where people go to be punished or rewarded after death. The *Kojiki* includes no commandments or explicit rules for how to live. It does not even say that people have to believe in the kami: it just tells the tales. The *Kojiki* also gives a genealogy (family tree) of the gods, which says that the emperor's family is descended from the kami of the sun. (The command to write the *Kojiki* was intended to strengthen the imperial family's right to rule at a time when Buddhism and other Chinese influences were emerging and the various tribes were not yet fully under the emperor's

理。玉之小琴之殊尓赤。古言乎。花勝見都

而不識有。後世之漢國意乃。所爲尓志有

祁礼婆。其訓状那母。佐比豆珠夜戒籍讀

之訓状尓旦掛麻久母阿夜尓畏伎風音

乃。遠皇祖之神之御代乃。雅言尓波不有

在祁流。故是以石上古學爲徒之夏野行

道之松陰余理旦宜伎可美本者奥津白

珠得迦旦尓斯有乎肥國人。長瀬真幸伊

其衰志母小松之末能憂念而。宣長之傳

尓余曽理旦父字乎母訓衰母伊勢海之

清波限之。清良祁久曰下乃山之直越路

○古事記所字

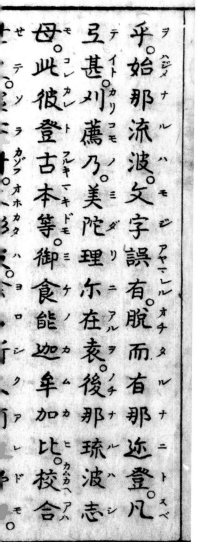

power. The book was meant to establish that the emperor wasn't just any kami but was descended from the most important kami.)

Unlike many other religions, Shinto was not and is not based on a holy book or on the agreement to believe certain stories or teachings. Shinto did not originate from a single person's beliefs or experiences. At the core of Shinto are the spiritual rites of washing and purification and offerings to the kami, such as food or tokens that have been bought at the shrines. These tokens usually accompany a prayer or a request. Shinto also has its roots in communal and family festivals celebrating the annual spring planting and fall harvest, as well as births and marriages. Because the kami are everywhere, in everything, Shinto honors and focuses on nature.

This idea of paying attention to nature is important because each kami has the power to be creative or destructive, gentle or fierce. The rituals help people avoid the destructive, angry aspects of the kami. They also help

The *Kojiki* — the "Record of Ancient Matters" — contains Shinto stories that were already old when they were written down in 712 CE by order of the emperor.

25

Before they enter a Shinto shrine, people purify themselves by washing in the river. Cleanliness and purification were important when this picture was painted in the late 1500s, and they are still an important part of Japanese culture.

people avoid the aggressive, destructive aspects of themselves. There is little sense in Japanese mythology of an ongoing fight between good and evil. Still, humans sometimes do wrong and must recognize these wrongs and purify themselves.

Shinto Myths

People had told some of these Shinto myths for centuries before they were written down. When they were documented in the *Kojiki*, they were written down for the emperor, at his command, at a time when Japan was reflecting on its relationship to Chinese and Korean cultures. The Shinto myths in the *Kojiki* are official versions, intended (among other things) to prove divinity of the emperor. But before that, there were already many written and oral versions of these myths. Even before writing, there was the *katari-be*, the "corporations of reciters," who had, however, become less important after the stories were documented in writing. As is often true, many versions of the myths existed. There wasn't necessarily a "right" one.

Buddhism

Buddhism was introduced in Japan in the sixth century CE when the Korean king sent the Japanese emperor a golden statue of the Buddha. Buddhism, by this time, was 1,000 years old and had already taken many forms in various regions throughout the world. Unlike Shinto, a Japanese tradition that had no specific founder or dogma, Buddhism

After Buddhism was introduced in Japan, it merged with Shinto. This statue of the Buddha, the religion's founder, is from the thirteenth century, when Buddhism was becoming more important in Japan.

had priests, many written texts, and well-defined beliefs. Central to these is the belief that people are meant to gain wisdom and eventually free themselves from the cycle of reincarnation—death and rebirth—and from a physical world of suffering.

It was Chinese Buddhism rather than the Korean form of Buddhism that was eventually accepted by the Japanese court and then by the people. Rather than replacing Shinto, however, Chinese Buddhism was absorbed and changed, as Japanese society adapts and reinterprets everything it learns from other cultures. If we imagine culture as a rich soup, then the addition of Chinese Buddhism in Japan wasn't like adding noodles, which are independent from the broth, but rather like adding an ingredient that becomes part of the broth itself. This combination of Shinto and Buddhism remains to this day. Buddhism added to Japanese religion a concept of an afterlife—a time when people are judged, then rewarded or punished. The lines between Buddhism and Shinto are often blurred. The merging of Buddhist and Shinto teachings is even referred to as Ryobu-Shinto, or "Double-Shinto."

Buddhism teaches personal salvation and escape from the cycle of life, death, and rebirth, but it split into various branches. Originally it taught that people must follow the teachings of the Buddha—the person who began the religion, who then became the subject of many myths. Another branch said that people could get help from innumerable smaller gods, though they are actually more like saints, or, in Japan, which adopted this form of Buddhism, like kami.

Buddhist Gods

Bodhi Dharma, an Indian monk who traveled to China, began Zen Buddhism. One day while practicing meditation, he fell asleep.

When he awoke, he was so angry with himself that he cut off his eyelids, ensuring that he would never sleep again. From his eyelids grew the first tea plants. Tea is sacred to Zen Buddhists; it also contains enough caffeine to help people not fall asleep. Although Bodhi Dharma is presumed to be a historical character, the myth resembles the Shinto myth in which the body parts of a dismembered god are transformed into foods that are essential to the culture.

There are three distinct Buddhist deities in Japan—Amida, Kannon, and Jizo—and they are considered gods of mercy. (There are also many other deities, though they are lesser known.) The first god, Amida (Buddha), has been passed down into Japanese culture from China. He is originally

Bodhi Dharma, the Indian founder of Zen Buddhism, has an un-Japanese appearance in this portrayal showing him with a bushy beard and eyebrows.

The Buddhist god Jizo *(left)* stands at the gates of hell, but he helps the souls of children who have died. Amida *(right)* is a god and a Buddha. His name means "infinite life," and he helps people be reborn into the heavenly land, not hell or a reincarnation on Earth.

derived from the Sanskrit figure Amitabha since India is the birth-place of Buddhism. Amida is a bodhisattva ("an enlightened being") who postponed the opportunity to obtain his own salvation until all humans had been saved.

The second god of mercy, Kannon, is another bodhisattva whose desire to protect humanity comes in the form of a postponed salvation. He is the god who protects children (and women during childbirth). Japanese Buddhists turn to Kannon for wisdom and counsel. Kannon is usually depicted as Senju Kannon, or the "Kannon of a Thousand Arms." These images are similar to those of Indian bodhisattvas with all of their arms outstretched in a pose showing their compassion. In Japan, Senju Kannon is also usually seen with a miniature Amida on his head. Kannon is sometimes depicted holding a lotus, or as a horse-headed figure with a third eye.

Jizo is the third Buddhist god of mercy. Like Kannon, he protects children, especially those who have died. Jizo also protects human souls who are in pain. Japanese Buddhists believe Jizo can redeem troubled souls from hell. Temples honoring Jizo are popular in Japan.

4 JAPANESE GODS AND GODDESSES

The Japanese say there are more than eight million or "800 myriad" kami. This isn't meant as a definite number. Eight million is another way of saying countless—or even infinite—since everything and everyone is a potential kami.

Of those countless kami, some are like the gods and goddesses of Greece, Rome, and Egypt. They are from a time before the world was modern, when the kami created and fought with one another, brought death into the world, and sometimes behaved in evil ways such as destroying irrigation ditches and murdering relatives. They also behaved

The heavenly deities Izanagi and Izanami stood on the "Bridge of Heaven" to create the first solid land. Hiroshige, one of Japan's greatest artists, created this image in 1850.

in ways that Japanese people are supposed to, such as purifying themselves with water. The tendency of gods to do horrific actions is just one of the things that has made myths interesting and confusing for thousands of years.

Sometimes it's helpful to think of the kami as demonstrating what Japanese should *not* do. Their misadventures show us what they can get away with—or not—but what we as mere humans most definitely cannot. Their behavior demonstrates that they are not of our modern world but rather of an earlier time. When a god goes into the underworld and gets into trouble, it tells us that we are supposed to leave the underworld untouched. We also learn what the culture's idea of the underworld is. In the case of the Japanese/Shinto myth, it is a place of impurity and decay.

The Heavenly Deities

Before there was breath or form, before heaven and earth were separated, before there were names, the first three kami came into existence. They were invisible. The earth looked like "floating oil" and "drifted like a jellyfish." Something like young reeds sprouted and from them two more invisible kami came forth. Since they are not visible, they are not described, but they are known as the Separate Heavenly Deities. Other deities followed, and they were all invisible (at least to humans). They are the gods of Takamagahara, or the "High Plains of Heaven."

The oldest of these gods was called Amanominakanushi-no-kami, or the "Lord of the Center of Heaven." Two other kami

of the High Plains of Heaven were called Takamimusubi and
Kamimusubi. These three kami, along with two lesser gods named
Umashiashikabihikoji-no-kami and Amanotokotachi-no-kami, formed
the five Separate Heavenly Deities, which were followed by seven
consecutive generations of heavenly gods and goddesses.

Izanagi and Izanami Create the World

The last two heavenly deities created were called Izanagi-no-mikoto
("The August—distinguished and grand—Male") and his sister and
wife, Izanami-no-mikoto ("The August Female"). The other heavenly
deities commanded them, "Complete and solidify the drifting land,"
and gave them the heavenly jeweled spear.

Izanagi and Izanami stood on the Heavenly Floating Bridge
(perhaps a rainbow, or the Milky Way). Reaching down, they
churned the primeval salt waters with the spear, making a churning
sound, *koworo korowo ni*. When they lifted the spear, the brine
dripped down and created solid land: the island of Onogoro.

Izanagi and Izanami descended from the heavens to this island
and built a pillar and a palace. They agreed to walk around the pillar,
Izanagi from the left and Izanami from the right. When they met,
Izanami spoke first. Then Izanagi spoke. But he was displeased. He
said the man should speak first. They soon had a child, but the child,
Hiruko, was a deformed creature, a "leech child," and they put it on
a boat made of reeds and floated it out to sea. (An ancient Japanese
ritual reflects this myth when after the birth of a couple's first child,
they place a clay figurine in a small reed boat and cast it out to sea.)

Izanagi and Izanami agreed to talk to the heavenly deities about what had gone wrong, and the deities performed a divination, heating the shoulder blade of a deer and examining the cracks that formed. The gods told them that the man should have spoken first. The birth of the demon child was the result of his mother having spoken out of turn during the ritual of courtship, a myth that some people today believe contributes to—or reflects—the inequalities between men and women in modern Japan.

After, Izanagi and Izanami went back to the island and performed the rite again, only this time Izanagi spoke first. Then Izanami gave birth to the eight islands of Japan. After that were born the kami that would inhabit and rule the islands. These included the gods of wind, the seas, the rivers, the trees, the mountains, the plains, the seasons, and many others.

This "wedded rock" shrine represents the marriage of Izanagi and Izanami. The rope must be replaced several times each year.

The thunder god *(right)* and wind god *(left)*, both weather deities, together create a big noisy wind storm.

The Death of Izanami

As Izanami gave birth to the kami of fire, Kagu-tsuchi, she was burned and became ill. In her death throes, she vomited up the gods of metal and mines. She urinated the gods of water and the green plants that grow in water. She excreted, and in her excrement were the gods of clay or earth. Afterward, she died and Izanagi buried her.

Izanagi wept and raged in his grief. "I have given away my beloved spouse in exchange for a mere child," he said. His tears became the kami whose name means "Weeping Marsh Woman." In his rage he took his sword and cut off the head of Kagu-tsuchi. From the fire god's blood and from all his body parts came other gods, known as the kami "born of sword." They are gods connected with fire and rocks, the gods of the volcano and of earthquakes.

Izanagi went to the land of the darkness, Yomi-tsu-kuni, the underworld, to seek his wife. When he found her, at the dark entrance of the underworld and shrouded in shadows, he said, "Oh, my beloved spouse, we have not finished making the lands. You must come back!" She backed away and warned Izanagi not to look at her.

It was too late. Izanami had already "eaten at the hearth," meaning she had eaten the food of the underworld. She said, however, that she would ask the gods of Yomi if she could return to earth and said again that Izanagi must not look upon her. But while she was away, he grew impatient and curious. A long time passed. He wanted so strongly to see his wife again that he broke off a tooth from the comb in his hair and used it as a torch. He went into the room where Izanami had gone and saw at once that she was a rotted corpse full of squirming maggots.

Izanagi was afraid and fled, but Izanami was angry at his having shamed her. She sent after him the hags of Yomi. Izanagi threw down the vine that held his hair and it bore grapes, which the hags stopped and ate. When they pursued him again, he pulled out the comb from his hair and threw it down. This time it bore bamboo shoots. Again the hags stopped and ate. Izanagi fled again, waving his sword behind him. He threw three peaches at his pursuers (which by now included the hags, the warriors of Yomi, and eight thunder deities that had formed in Izanami's body) and asked them to save him, which they did.

Izanami herself chased after him then, but he escaped and moved a huge rock to block the pass between them. They broke their wedding vows, divorcing. Izanami swore that she would kill 1,000 people a day, and Izanagi swore that he would cause 1,500 births each day, accounting for human mortality and for population increase.

Izanami became kami of the world of death. It is not a place of punishment or judgment in Shinto myth, but a place of darkness, decay, and pollution (in the sense of ritual uncleanliness).

The Birth of the Sun and Moon

Izanagi said, "I have been to a most horrid, unclean land. I must purify myself." (Traditionally, the Japanese still take a ritual bath after a period of mourning.) At the mouth of a stream in Hyuga (northeast Kyushu), Izanagi took off his clothing, out of which were born many kamis, and he bathed. From his bathing, other deities were born. The last three were the most important. When he bathed his left eye, Amaterasu-no-mikoto, the sun was born, literally "August [important] Person Who Makes the Heavens Shine." When he bathed his right eye, Tsuki-yomi-no-mikoto ("the August Moon") was born. And when he washed his nose, Susano-no-mikoto ("the August Raging Male") was born.

Izanagi rejoiced at these three noble children and he gave his power to them. He decided to divide the earth and give each god a portion of it. To Amaterasu, he gave a jangling necklace and said, "You shall rule the High Plains of Heaven."

To Tsuki, he said, "You shall rule realm of the night."

To Susano, he said, "You shall rule the ocean," although Susano is also the kami of storms, which come from the ocean.

大日本名将鑑

天照皇大神天の巌戸隠させ
たまひ世の中常闇のやみとなり
ければ八百萬の神たち巌戸の
前に集ひ神いさめの神楽を奏
し白女命神楽を舞給ひければ
面白やとて天手力雄命其戸を
取て投ぬれば遠かみ飛び
止るに依て戸隠明神と申し奉る

In the Japanese creation myth, the sun goddess, Amaterasu, is
lured from the cave where she has hidden herself by the sounds
of a noisy dance.

Obediently, Amaterasu and Tsuki went to rule the realms that had been given to them, but Susano wept and howled, until mountain vegetation died and the rivers and seas dried up. (He seems to have been using up the world's water, not adding to it, as a storm would later.) His father asked him, "Why do you weep and howl instead of ruling the land entrusted to you?" "I wish to go to the land of my mother," Susano answered.

Angry, Inazagi banished Susano, saying, "You may not live in this land." This last myth has two endings. In one, Susano ascended to heaven where he remains in the Younger Palace of the Sun. In the other version of this myth, Susano is enshrined at Taga (in Shiga Prefecture, Honshu).

Susano Challenges His Sister

Susano said that if he was banished, he first wanted to visit his sister, Amaterasu. When he went up there, the mountains and rivers roared. The land shook. Hearing this, the sun goddess believed her brother was coming to take her lands, and she prepared herself for battle. She tied her long hair in bunches and put on two quivers of arrows, one containing 1,000 arrows and another containing 500 arrows. She put on the arm guard that protects the arm from the string of the bow, and she stomped on the earth, sinking to her thighs, kicking the earth as if it were light snow.

"Why have you come?" she asked her brother.

Susano said that he had no ill intentions, but Amaterasu wasn't certain if she should believe him. They agreed to a contest that involved each of them bearing children.

Amaterasu asked for Susano's sword. She broke it in three pieces, washed it, and then chewed the pieces and spat out three goddesses. Susano asked for the string of many beads that Amaterasu wore in her hair, chewed them up, and spat out a male god. He did the same with the vines in her hair and the beads on her arms.

Who won? They couldn't agree. Susano had produced the male children, but since he had used things belonging to Amaterasu, she claimed they were hers. He, however, argued that the contest was to prove him pure of heart. His having helped produce the first three "graceful maidens" proved this.

Susano then had a kind of victory rage. He broke down the ridges between his sister's rice paddies and covered up the irrigation ditches. He defecated and scattered his feces in the hall where the first fruits were tasted.

Susano generally causes trouble in the myths, but he does kill an eight-headed dragon (mostly hidden in the raging waters in this scroll painting) and rescue the princess Kushinada.

Amaterasu did not scold him, perhaps hoping to calm him, but it didn't help. Susano then took a heavenly pony (probably a piebald, dappled one, which in many cultures is thought to resemble the stars), skinned it backward, and then heaved it through the roof of the heavenly weaving hall where his sister was working. A weaving maiden was so startled that she injured herself and died.

The Sun Conceals Herself

Amaterasu was afraid, and she hid herself in a cave or house of rocks, the Heavenly Rock Cave, or Ama-no-iwato. The High Plain of the Heavenly Deities and the Central Land of the Reed Plains— the world of human beings—were in darkness. There was only night. The voices of the kami rose in alarm and terrible things happened.

Omopi-kane-no-kami thought about the problem. (*Omopo* literally means "to ponder," and this kami is always the one called upon to come up with ideas for the heavenly kamis. His whole name suggests that he is "thought-combining-kami," able to hold many thoughts, or to think with many kamis.) Eventually the kami constructed a large mirror and suspended it from the branches of a sacred tree taken from the mountains. They hung white and blue cloth in the tree. At the top of the tree was a perch (whose shape became the shape of a Shinto shrine) with a rooster on it. One kami held up the tree while another spoke solemn words of magic. Then a beautiful kami, Ama-no-uzume, stood on an upside-down bucket and danced, exposing her body, until all the eighty myriad kami laughed. (She wasn't performing a nightclub act, but rather the dance of a female shaman, a woman of magic power.)

Amaterasu cracked open the door and said, "I thought that the lands would be dark. Why is Ama-no-uzume singing and dancing and all of you laughing?"

Ama-no-uzume said they were laughing because there was a kami superior even to Amaterasu. Two gods held the mirror facing the door of the cave where Amaterasu was hiding. As she emerged and approached the mirror, it was as if a ray of dawn had broken. A god who had concealed himself, a god of great strength, pulled her out; another god extended a magic rope behind her, saying "You may go back no further than this!"

And so, with the sun's reappearance, the light came back into the world, as the sun comes out after darkness, after the storm of her storm brother's actions. Amaterasu had restored sunlight to the world.

The eighty myriad kami punished Susano severely, making him pay a fine of a thousand tables of ritual offerings. They also cut off his long beard and his fingernails and toenails, and forced him from heaven, sending him back to earth. When he returned, he got into more trouble, although eventually he killed an eight-headed dragon by getting it so drunk on rice wine (sake) that he could chop it up. While hacking up its tail, he discovered in it a sword that appears in many other Japanese myths.

Replicas of that sword, the mirror that was used to entice Amaterasu from hiding, and the beads that Amaterasu wore in her hair, from which Susano created children, are given to each new Japanese emperor when he is enthroned. They are the three insignia of kingship that tie the emperor to the gods, and especially to Amaterasu, from whom the emperor is descended.

Other Shinto Gods

The Shinto religion includes other gods not mentioned in the previous myths. Okuninushi, "the Great Lord of the Country," had eighty brothers, and all of them, including Okuninushi, wanted to marry the princess Ya-gami-hime. On their way to court the princess, the brothers saw a rabbit with no fur weeping from pain at the side of the road. The brothers told the rabbit that he must bathe in salt water and dry himself in the wind on a mountain. This, of course, hurt the rabbit even more. Okuninushi told the rabbit to bathe in the sweet water at the mouth of the river and to roll in a particular kind of pollen. The rabbit, a god in disguise, was cured and promised Okuninushi that he would wed the princess.

There are many stories about Okuninushi, some of which pit him against Susano, whom he finally overcomes. While Susano is asleep, Okuninushi ties his long hair to the rafters of the palace.

Ogetsu-no-hime is a goddess of food. In different versions of the myth, either Tsukiyomi (the moon god) or Susano is given food by Inari. The food comes from her whole body—it comes out her mouth, her nose, even her rectum. Offended, the other god kills her. From her dead body come silkworms, rice, millet, red beans, wheat, and soybeans—essential products in traditional Japanese life.

When this myth is told of the moon god (as it is in the *Nihon Shoki*, the "Chronicles of Japan," written shortly after the *Kojiki*), it can account for why the moon was banished to the dark sky: after his act of destruction, the sun says she never wants to see him again.

Other gods include Inari, the rice god who ensures a bountiful rice harvest and is also considered the god of prosperity. Ebisu is the kami who is the god of work. The Japanese even have a deity to oversee kitchen appliances! Kamado-no-kami is the god of kitchen ranges. Truly, the Japanese world is full of kami.

Shinto Demons

Shinto, like many other world religions, has its equivalent of hell, partly acquired from Buddhism. This dark realm is called Jigoku, and it consists of eight regions of fire and eight regions of ice. The ruler of Jigoku is known as Emma-ho. He is the one responsible for judging the souls of male sinners, condemning them to one of the sixteen regions for punishment. His sister judges female sinners. As a ritual of punishment, each sinner stands before a mirror where his or her sins are reflected back at him or her. But the souls of sinners can also be saved. This salvation requires intervention by a bosatsu or by bodhisattva kami.

Emma-ho, ruler of the Shinto equivalent of hell, can assign dead sinners to eight regions of fire and eight of ice.

Demons that inhabit both Jigoku and Earth are known as *oni*. These demons cause events such as tragic storms, fires, epidemics of disease, famine, and other catastrophes involving large losses of life. Some oni can even take on a human or animal form, though most are invisible.

5 MYTHOLOGY IN MODERN JAPAN

The myths in this book are ancient, and neither Shinto nor Buddhism were or are primarily religions based on the retelling of myths. Most reference books about modern Japan claim that religion is not a very important part of the lives of the Japanese. Yet Akihito, who became emperor in 1989, traces his family back more than 2,600 years to the emperor Jimmu, and thus to the sun goddess. In October 2005, Prime Minister Junichiro Koizumi of Japan angered other Asian nations by visiting Yasukuni Shrine in Tokyo at which the Japanese who died in wars are "memorialized and worshipped as deities"— including soldiers who were executed as

This brightly painted doll represents a samurai warrior and is used in Kabuki theater.

war criminals. The dead become kami, even if they have done terrible things.

Today, the most important annual event at every Japanese shrine is the annual festival called the *gion matsuri*. During this celebration, men and women of the community carry an image of the local shrine around the neighborhood in order to sanctify both it and the local people. The myths and the traditions and ceremonies that go with them still affect modern Japanese life and culture in all sorts of ways. Many Japanese observe Shinto customs but are buried according to Buddhist

In modern Japan, young men still honor their local shrine by carrying an image of it around the neighborhood during the gion matsuri festival.

rituals. The Japanese appreciation of nature, their emphasis on cleanliness and on purification, and the discipline they bring to play and work are all related to Shinto and Buddhist traditions.

There is a popular saying in Japan: 80 percent of the people of Japan say they are Buddhist, 80 percent say they are Shinto, and 80 percent say they believe in no religion at all. The Japanese blend of Buddhism and Shinto is less about belief than it is about acting in certain ways—meditating, visiting Buddhist temples and Shinto jinta, or shrines. (Most houses contain both types.) Most weddings are Shinto. Most funerals are Buddhist.

Both traditions emphasize ritual purification: you wash out your mouth and wash your hands before visiting a shrine. And a lot of shrine visiting and ritual blessings go on. When the ground is broken for a new building, there is a ceremony to pacify the kami who dwell there and to purify the place. New airplanes are purified before their first flight and so are new cars on a factory assembly line. Toyota executives travel three hours from their headquarters to unveil their newest cars at the shrine of the sun goddess, Amaterasu.

In a modern Shinto-style wedding, the bride and groom pass a ceremonial cup of sake (rice wine) back and forth three times, taking a sip each time.

On the first business day of the year, these businessmen are at the Shinto shrine of commerce and industry, where the priest performs a ritual blessing.

The myths aren't as important as they once were, but Japanese tradition goes on—with some typically Japanese modifications. A shrine visit still includes washing, ringing a bell (to summon the kami), bowing twice, and clapping the hands two times before giving an offering. Few Japanese communities are without their own Shinto shrine; they number more than 80,000 throughout the country. You can still get your fortune on a piece of paper at a shrine. If it's good, you keep it, and if it's bad, you leave it tied near the shrine, where the kami will make it go away. The modern difference is that now you can buy your fortune from a vending machine.

GLOSSARY

Age of Enlightenment A period during the eighteenth century known as the European Age of Reason because of the progress made in the academic fields of philosophy and ethics.

anthropologist A person who studies the origin and behavior of human beings and their cultures.

august Majestic; full of grandeur.

Buddhism A religion that is based upon the teachings of Siddhartha Gautama and that originated in India more than 2,500 years ago. Buddhism spread from India to China and then into Japan.

deity A god or supreme being.

dharma In Buddhism, the body of teachings expounded by Buddha; the principle or law that orders the universe.

divine To emanate from God; to have God-like qualities.

dogma A religious claim that must be believed but cannot be proved.

hierarchy A system of ranking.

homogeneous Consisting of the same kind; uniform.

kami A Japanese word meaning "god" or "goddess" or "spirit."

nationalism Loyalty to a nation or ethnicity over all others.

ritual A custom or practice often associated with a religious observance.

samurai The military aristocracy of ancient Japan.

Shinto The ancient Japanese religion that finds sacredness in everything.

shogunate The military government that ruled Japan until the restoration of the emperor in 1867.

shrine A holy or sacred place that is dedicated to a god, goddess, saint, or religious martyr.

temple A place of worship for Buddhists, Hindus, and Jews.

FOR MORE INFORMATION

The American Folklore Society
Merchon Center
The Ohio State University
1501 Neil Avenue
Columbus, OH 43201
(614) 191-3375
Web site: http://www.afsnet.org

Asian Art Museum of San Francisco
200 Larkin Street
San Francisco, CA 94102
(415) 581-3500
Wed site: http://www.asianart.org

Asia Society
725 Park Avenue (at 70th Street)
New York, NY 10021
(212) 288-6400
Web site: http://www.asiasociety.org

Japan Society
333 East Forty-seventh Street
New York, NY 10017
(212) 832-1155
Web site: http://www.japansociety.org

Los Angeles County Museum of Art
5905 Wilshire Boulevard
Los Angeles, CA 90036
(323) 857-6000
Web site: http://www.lacma.org

The Metropolitan Museum of Art
1000 Fifth Avenue
New York, NY 10028
(212) 535-7710
Web site: http://www.metmuseum.org

Web Sites

Due to the changing nature of Internet links, Rosen Publishing has developed an online list of Web sites related to the subject of this book. This site is updated regularly. Please use this link to access the list:

http://www.rosenlinks.com/maw/japa

FOR FURTHER READING

Ashkenazi, Michael. *Handbook of Japanese Mythology* (Handbook of World Mythology). Santa Barbara, CA: ABC-CLIO, 2003.

Avakian, Monique. *The Meiji Restoration and the Rise of Modern Japan*. Glenview, IL: Silver Burdett Press, 1991.

Blumberg, Rhoda. *Commodore Perry in the Land of the Shogun*. New York, NY: HarperCollins, 1985.

Davis, F. Hadland. *Myths and Legends of Japan*. Mineola, NY: Dover Publications, 1992.

Hartz, Paula. *Shinto* (World Religions). Updated ed. New York, NY: Facts on File, 2004.

Haugaard, Erik. *The Boy and the Samurai*. New York, NY: Houghton Mifflin, 1991.

McAlpine, Helen, and William McAlpine. *Tales from Japan* (Oxford Myths and Legends). New York, NY: Oxford University Press, 2002.

Nishmimura, Shigeo. *An Illustrated History of Japan*. New York, NY: Tuttle, 2005.

Patterson, Katherine. *The Master Puppeteer*. New York, NY: Crowell, 1975.

Patterson, Katherine. *Of Nightingales That Weep*. New York, NY: HarperCollins, 1989.

Patterson, Katherine. *The Sign of the Chrysanthemum*. New York, NY: HarperCollins, 1988.

Phillips, Douglas A., Charles F. Gritzner, and Kristi L. Desaulniers. *Japan* (Modern World Nations). New York, NY: Chelsea House, 2003.

Piggott, Juliet. *Japanese Mythology* (Library of the World's Myths and Legends). New York, NY: Peter Bedrick, 1991.

Roberts, Jeremy. *Japanese Mythology A to Z* (Mythology A to Z). New York, NY: Facts on File, 2003.

Tyler, Royall. *Japanese Tales*. New York, NY: Pantheon, 2002.

Wangu, Madhu Bazaz. *Buddhism* (World Religions). 3rd ed. New York, NY: Facts on File, 2006.

Willis, Roy, ed. *World Mythology*. New York, NY: Henry Holt and Company, 1993.

BIBLIOGRAPHY

Ashkenazi, Michael. *Handbook of Japanese Mythology* (Handbook of World Mythology). Santa Barbara, CA: ABC-CLIO, 2003.

Barthes, Roland. *An Empire of Signs*. New York, NY: Hill & Wang, 1982.

Brunvand, Jan Harold. *The Study of American Folklore: An Introduction*. 4th ed. New York, NY: W. W. Norton and Co., 1998.

Davis, F. Hadland. *Myths and Legends of Japan*. Mineola, NY: Dover Publications, 1992.

Feiler, Bruce S. *Learning to Bow: Inside the Heart of Japan*. New York, NY: Ticknor and Fields, 1991.

Hartz, Paula. *Shinto* (World Religions). Updated ed. New York, NY: Facts on File, 2004.

Jung, Carl Gustav, and Carl Kerenyi. *Essays on a Science of Mythology*. Princeton, NJ: Princeton University Press, 1980.

Kirk, G. S. *Myth: Its Meaning and Functions in Ancient and Other Cultures*. Berkeley, CA: University of California Press, 1973.

Ono, Sokyo. *Shinto: The Kami Way*. New York, NY: Tuttle, 1962.

Oring, Elliott. *Folk Groups and Folklore Genres: An Introduction*. Salt Lake City, UT: Utah State University Press, 1986.

Piggott, Juliet. *Japanese Mythology* (Library of the World's Myths and Legends). New York, NY: Peter Bedrick, 1991.

Varley, H. Paul. *Japanese Culture*. 3rd ed. Honolulu, HI: University of Hawaii Press, 1984.

Wangu, Madhu Bazaz. *Buddhism* (World Religions). 3rd ed. New York, NY: Facts on File, 2006.

INDEX

About the Author

Judith Levin studied folklore in a Ph.D. program at the University of Pennsylvania, where she learned about mythology as well as other aspects of folklore and cross-cultural studies. She is the author of many books for children and young adults, including a biography of Ichiro Suzuki, who is the first Japanese position player (a player other than a pitcher) to come to U.S. major league baseball.

Photo Credits